#UNICORNLIFE
A FUNNY UNICORN COLORING BOOK FOR ADULTS

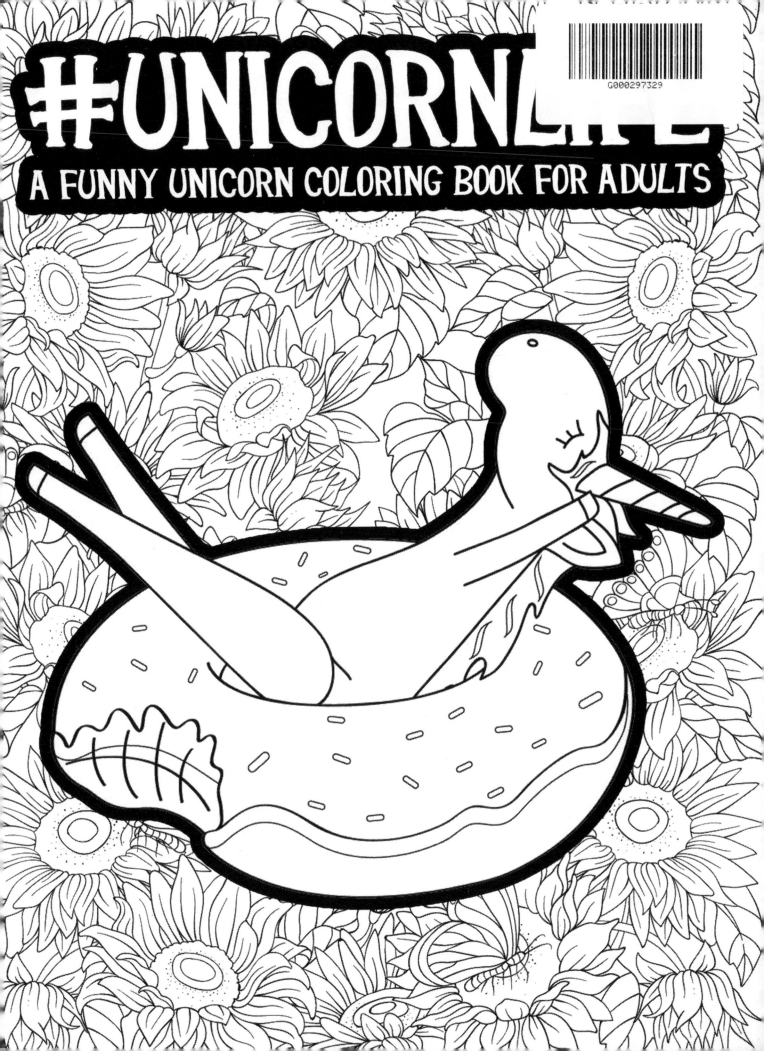

G000297329

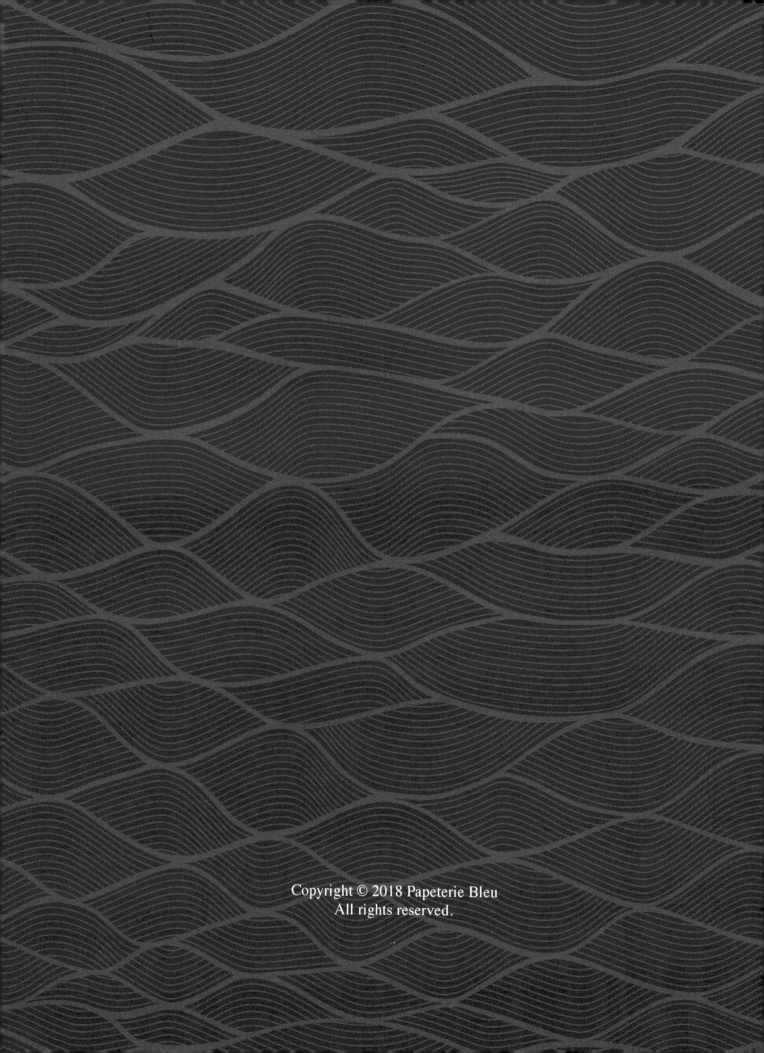

FREE DOWNLOAD

www.papeteriebleu.com/unicorn

YOUR DOWNLOAD CODE: UNN3893

 @papeteriebleu

 Papeterie Bleu

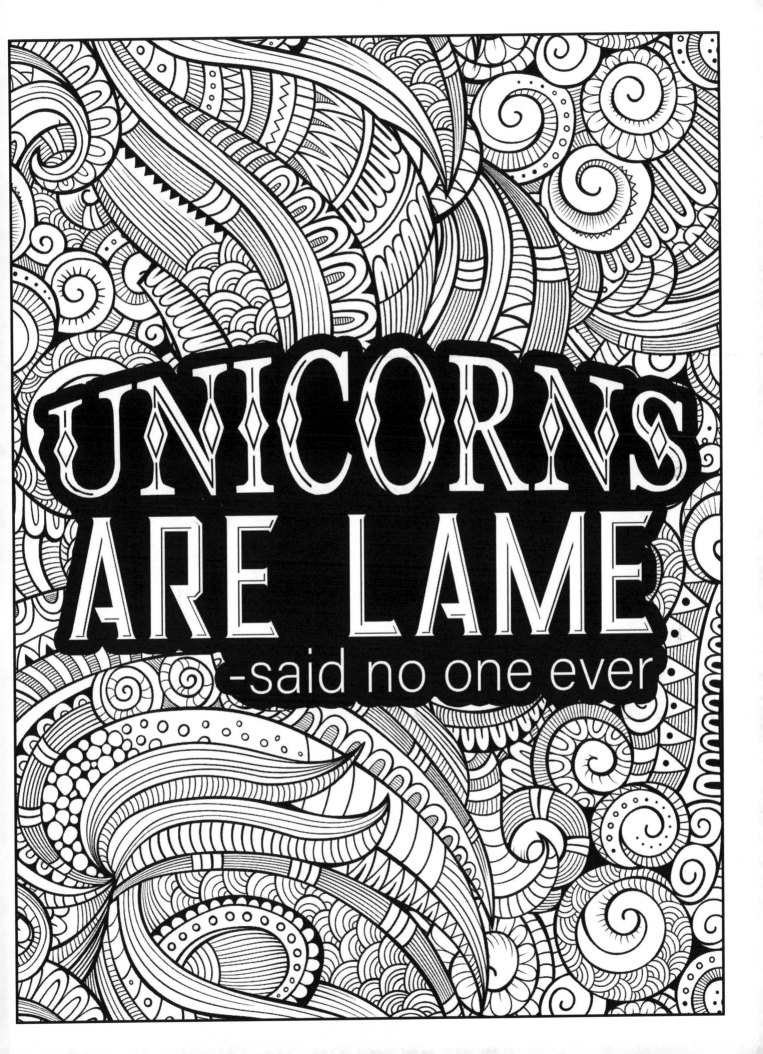

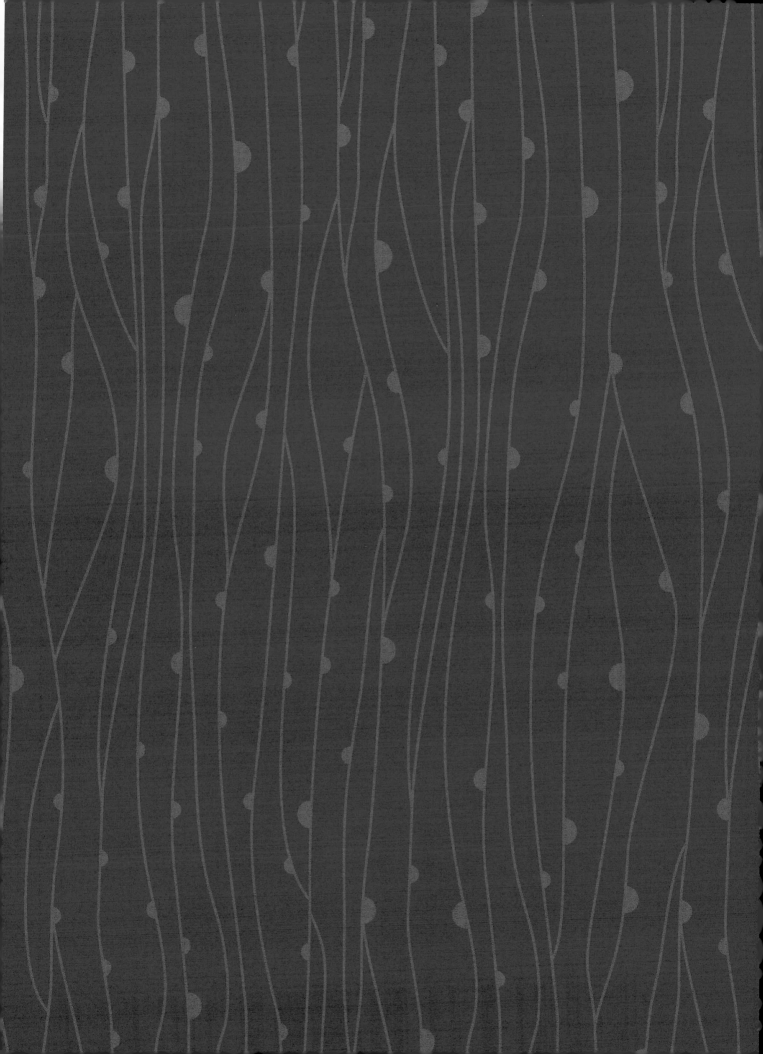

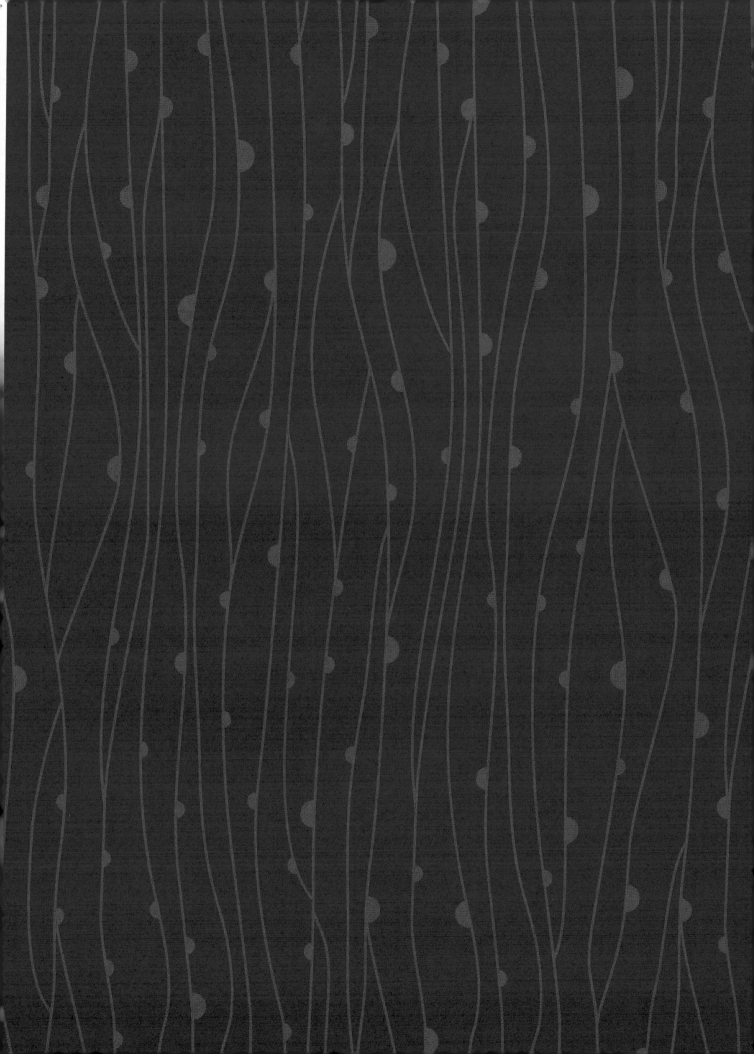

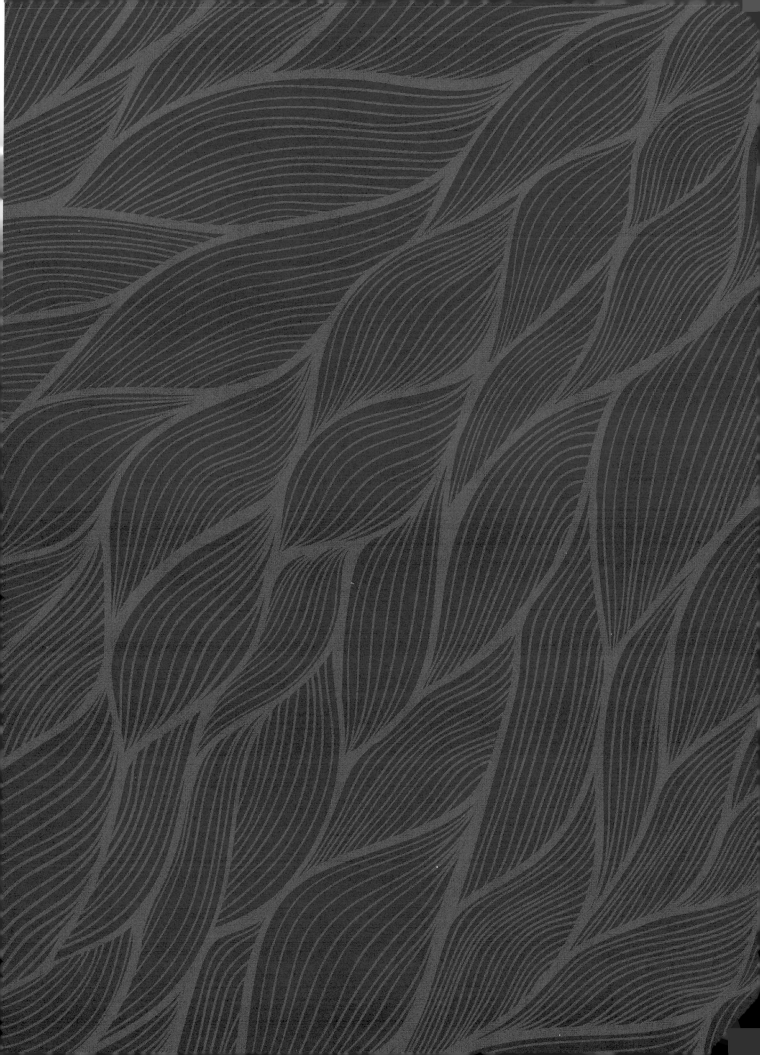

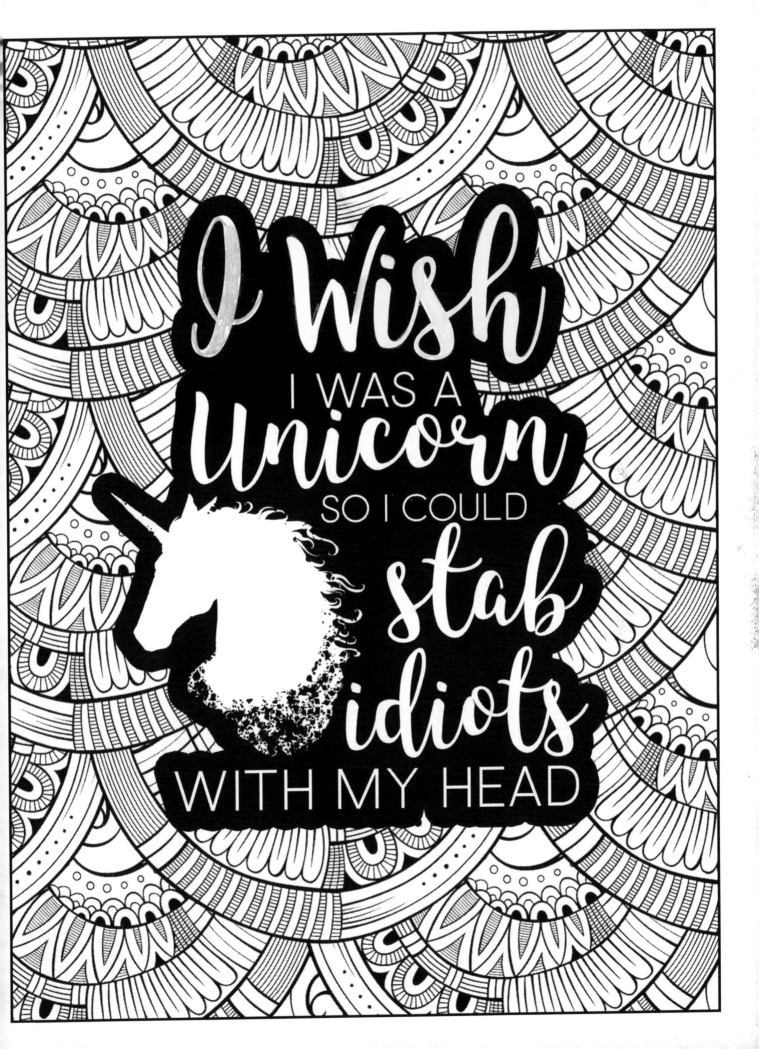

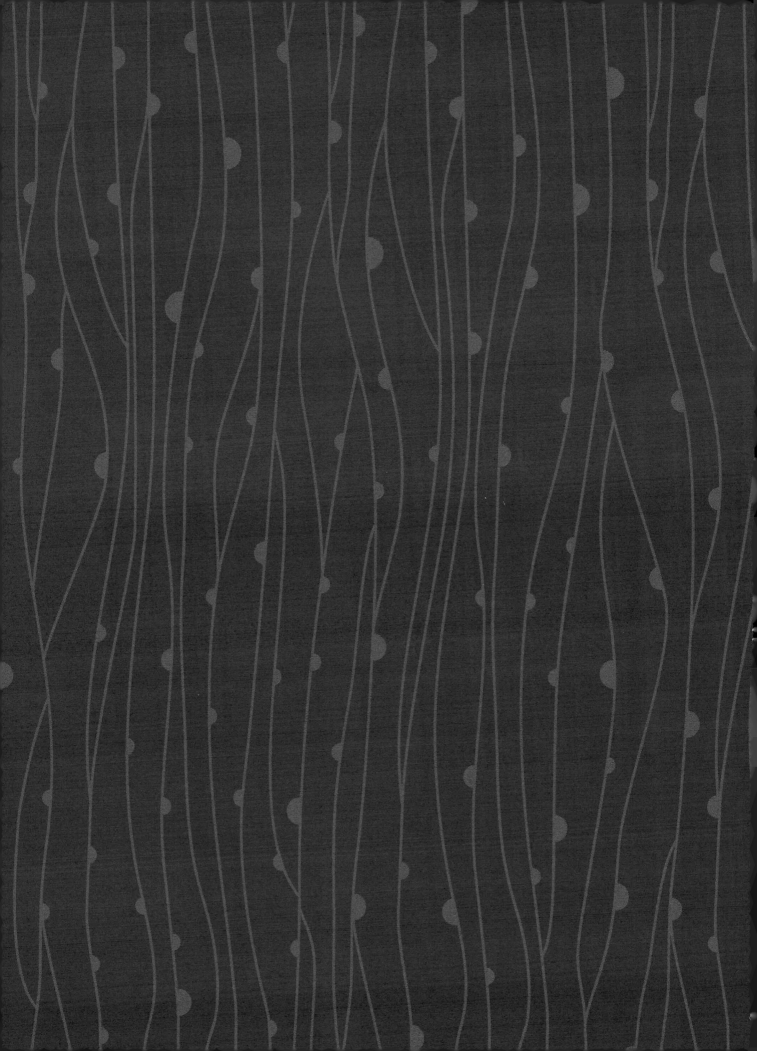

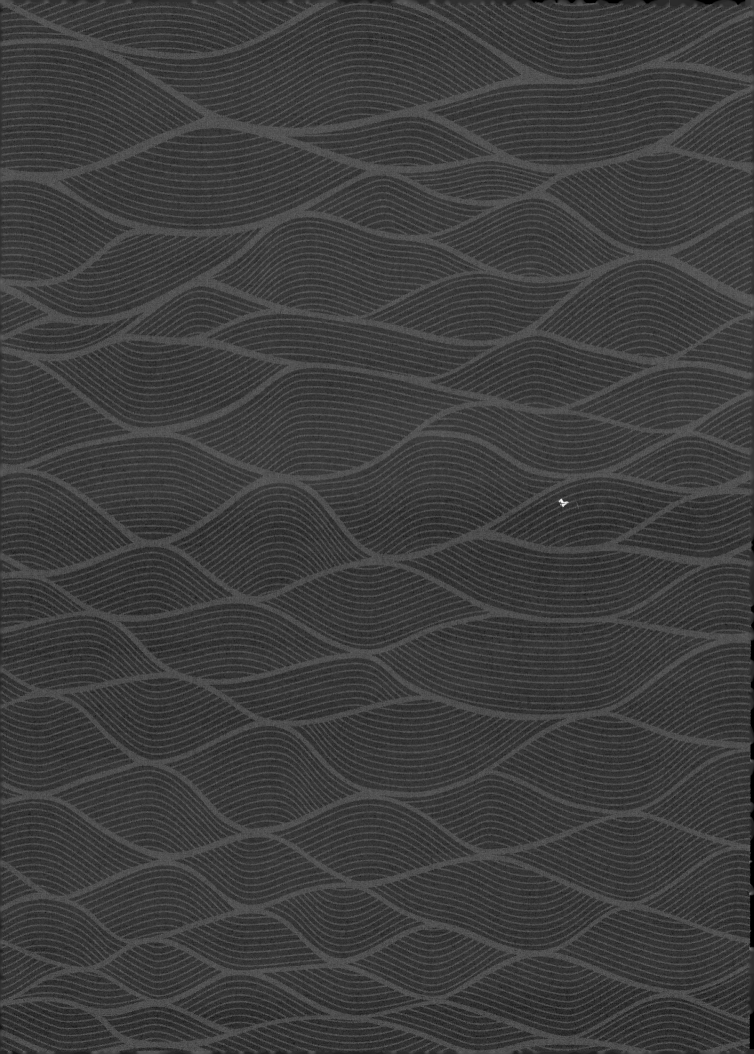

BE SURE TO FOLLOW US
ON SOCIAL MEDIA FOR THE
LATEST NEWS, SNEAK
PEEKS, & GIVEAWAYS

[instagram icon] @PapeterieBleu

[facebook icon] Papeterie Bleu

[twitter icon] @PapeterieBleu

ADD YOURSELF TO OUR MONTHLY
NEWSLETTER FOR FREE DIGITAL
DOWNLOADS AND DISCOUNT CODES

www.papeteriebleu.com/newsletter

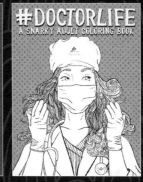

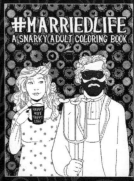

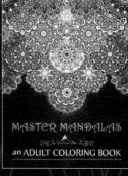

CHECK OUT OUR OTHER BOOKS!

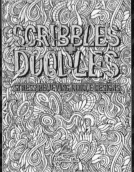

Made in the
USA
Columbia, SC